AF472296

Codex Terra Publishing

Poems One

Johnny D

ISBN 978-1-8479967-3-2
Poetry

This first edition is published by Codex Terra Publishing
Published in March 2008

Printed in England

Acknowledgements

There are a few quotes printed here, from William Shakespeare, Dylan Thomas and R.S. Thomas. In Haiku XXXIII there is a reference to Dorian Gray by Oscar Wilde. The title 'Time Enough for Love' is from a novel by Robert Heinlein. These are of course acknowledged as being the work of the respective authors.

Thanks to Michael Clift for reading through the whole collection and providing useful comments back to me. I hope to do the same for him soon…

Thanks to my wife Emily for her encouragement, her patience and her love.

JOHNNY D

POEMS ONE

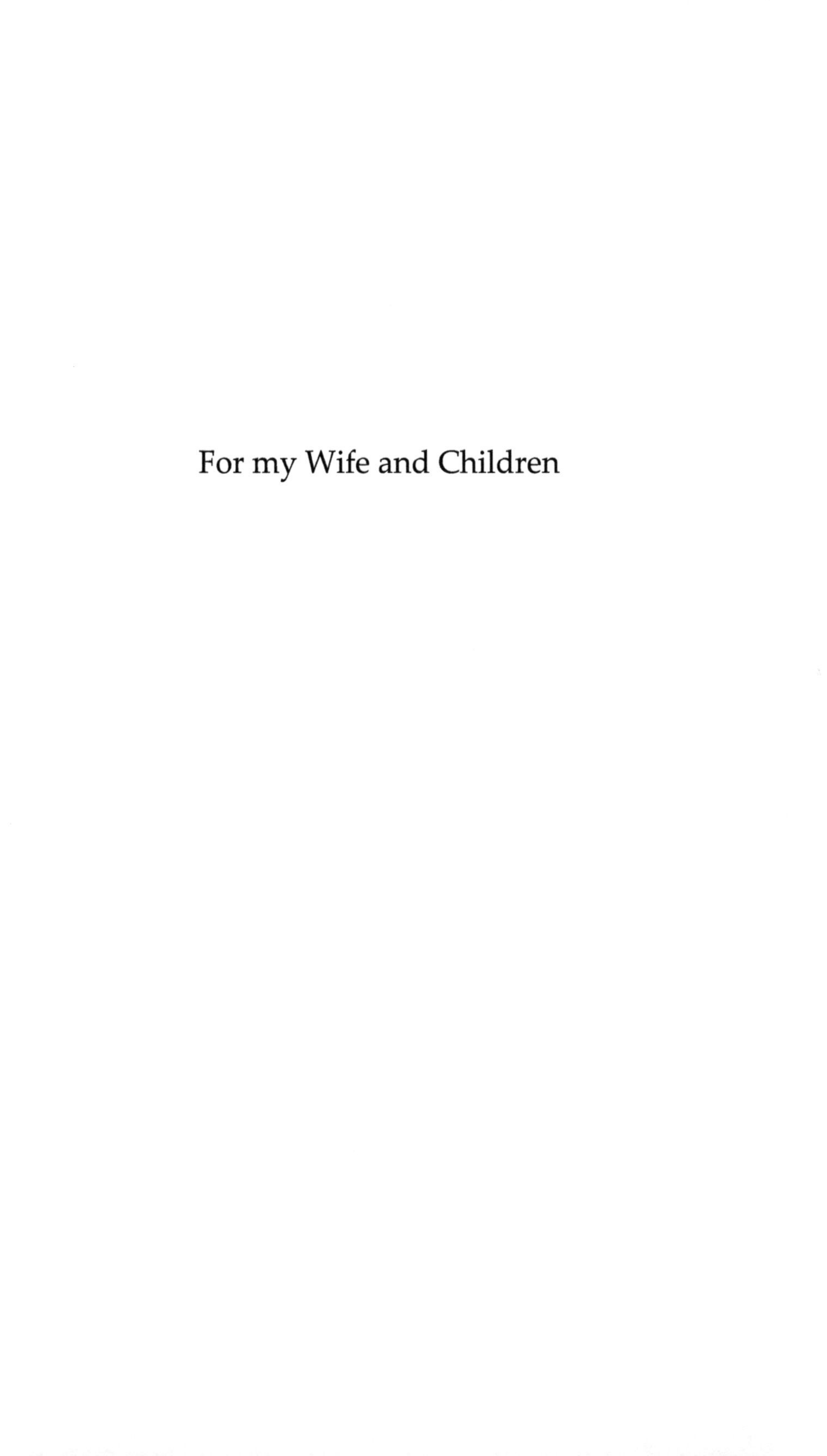

For my Wife and Children

CONTENTS

CONTENTS

CONTENTS

INTRODUCTION

This is a selection of my poems from the last ten years. I made this selection using two criteria: firstly I chose poems which I like, and secondly I added poems which other people said they liked. Sometimes the two coincide, and sometimes not. Erudite readers will notice immediately that there are a lot of Haiku in the selection, and the pedant in me feels the need to point out some Haiku facts.

The Haiku form originates in Japan, and on the simplest level is a poem in three parts, arranged in five, seven and five syllables – a seventeen syllable poem thus. However, the story is a lot more complicated than that, and you really need to be steeped in Japanese history and culture to understand even some of it. There are seasonal words, cutting words, and many other guidelines and traditions which influence the creation of a Haiku. Of course, the practised Haiku poet could break all of them and still come up with the goods, but as with any other discipline you need to know the rules in order to break them.

Another Japanese form is the Senryu. This bears a striking resemblance to a Haiku (it looks exactly the same). However, it is regarded as a form which has more freedom to it, often lighter in sentiment or even humorous. A lot of my Haiku are Senryu, and there also a few in a form called Tanka which is five-seven-five-seven-seven. In some respects, the whole idea of Haiku and Senryu in English is a bit of a stretch, as the way they are written in Japanese depends on puns and double-meanings as well as other devices.

I am told that Japanese lends itself to these very well, because of the way syllables can be re-used in a way which they cannot in English. I don't know for certain, as I do not speak Japanese. What I write is a seventeen syllable English poem, arranged following Haiku structural rules where appropriate. I also chain them together sometimes to make a longer poem.

Why do I do this? Mainly because I love the way this limitation forces me to think more about each and every word in the poem. It is also a form of poetry that works well in an age where the attention span of many people (myself included) is often the length of an SMS text message or a short email. I like Haiku and have fun writing them. I often write them on a mobile phone when I am on the move, and email them to myself for later editing. I really think the Haiku is an ideal poetic form for the 21st century!

Of course, not all the poems are Haiku or Senryu…

JOHNNY D

POEMS ONE

EPITAPH FOR A HOMELESS MAN

Shocked, with dread,
I realise that he is dead.
A crumpled bundle of dirty rags
Surrounded by old shopping bags.
Nobody there to mourn or pray
Lost, he simply died today.
Westminster workers, veiled and gloved
Don't question why he died unloved.
They roll him into a body bag,
'Unknown' scrawled on his toe tag.
Did he choose to drop dead here?
With parliament sitting so near?
Or was it an accident of fate
That dumped his corpse by government's gate?

HAIKU DIARY

I

A lifetime searching -
All this lovely knowledge gone.
A sigh in the wind.

II

Ancient charming face
Lit with a villainous smile.
A fallen angel.

III

Primeval Power,
Love can tear you apart
And it can heal you.

IV

Loud raucous laughter
In my neighbour's house. He is
A selfish bastard.

V

A man sees his youth
Reflected in a mirror
As a young man speaks

THE GREAT PRETENDER

The Great Pretender, his head in the clouds,
Laughing and waving at imaginary crowds.
He peddles an image as thin as tin –
Everyone knows that the image is not him.

The Great Pretender, a man of our times,
Gives his message of joy in a few email lines.
His big-jawed moon face with a fossilised grin,
Stares from a newsletter (which is in my bin).

The Great Pretender has no soul at all
Just a spin-doctored shell about six feet tall.
He has no idea what normal folk do –
Though maybe some day he will meet one or two.

VI

Joy blooms in stillness.
Happiness is here and now..
Use your eyes and ears.

VII

Wakeful, thoughtful, tired.
Grey mist beween tall buildings
Everything is vague

VII

Pig in the middle
They all want to let my blood.
Prey becomes hunter.

IX

This warm spring morning
Heralds the long summer days,
Though not in England.

X

My son sprawled in bed
Just visible in the dark
His life is precious

BETHLEHEM - FIVE LINKED HAIKU

I wrote this after reading about violence in Bethlehem, with Israeli soldiers pushing around Palestinian teenagers. The whole thing was depressing, pointless and vicious.

Inhumanity
Sidling through ruined houses.
Battered Bethlehem.

Arrogant soldiers
Pushing teenagers around.
Shots fired in the night.

My God is silent.
Perhaps he is in mourning.
Pointless deaths, daily.

People are stupid.
Avarice eats into them,
Chewing up their souls.

Gloom, black gloom, dark soul.
Fear, virus feeds on spirit.
A small death moment

10th April 2002

XI

There was sun today
The garden warm and golden
For a few minutes

XII

I fear the future
When I look into the past.
Man has not changed much.

XIII

To battle again.
Tomorrow the lines will form.
We fight for nothing.

XIV

Grass grows and grass dies.
Under a grey sky I stand
Watching the grass die.

XV

Raining again, but
Quietly. Whispering in
The background. Silence.

IN LONDON

I flew to London, going to meetings I did not want to attend. London was covered in grey cloud, very low hanging cloud, ominous cloud. Looking out of the aircraft window I imagined wild geese flying in the distance.

Early morning light
Wild geese flying silently
Across the grey sky

London is utterly commercial. Everywhere you look there are adverts trying to sell you stuff. On the tube I was disturbed by an advert that blatantly suggested you should put your home at risk to borrow large sums of money. Are people really so gullible? Other adverts for insurance, reduced phone rates, beer, share selling, food and some kind of herbal drug to keep you active. All of them uninspired and unattractive, boorish and artless. I am amazed that this crap can persuade people to want what they offer. There was a small ray of hope when I saw a poster for poems on the underground.

Nothing beautiful
In these caves under London.
Just ugly and sad.

Noisy young women,
Talking soap opera, sex
And bad hangovers.

XVI

Water bestows life
On this small black rock. Once dust,
Now it shines brightly.

XVII

Tiny little snail
Stuck to the window. Why did
It go there anyway?

XVIII

Sitting at my desk
Staring at some paperwork.
What nonsense it is.

XIX

Fear is a killer.
Every time you are afraid,
You die a little.

XX

In the smallest bud,
Life demonstrates its great strength.
It seems eternal.

TRAVELLING TO BROOMFIELD

White foam and seagulls.
The lowlands sink in the haze
And we journey on.

Green leaves hide the sky.
Fragile blue flowers carpet
The ground beneath them.

Grass cuttings piled high.
The smell of them fills the air -
Summer already?

Under the old oak -
Pale white petals all over,
Shining in the gloom.

XXI

All these moments will
Become memories, dream-like.
What is the present?

XXII

The past was once the
Future. Present becomes past
Immediately.

XXIII

Seagull sitting still
On the howling wind, riding
In his element.

XXIV

Blue and white and blue -
An infinite sky above.
Grey wings hanging there.

XXV

Soul-sick at leaving
Family and friends behind.
My endless journey.

TOGETHER

Just the two of us
Eating together tonight -
Should be more often.

TIME ENOUGH FOR LOVE

It takes a lifetime
To know what love is
A lifetime with open eyes
Open heart and mind.
Even then, it's a thin
Recognition.
So few know love.
So few receive it.

XXVI

Guttural cracked voice,
Incomprehensible sounds
From a nearby seat.

XXVII

The final brush stroke
Completes my work for the day.
Sitting, drinking tea.

XXVIII

How I love the spring.
Blossom on the neighbour's tree,
Warm sun on my back.

XXIX

Planning the future,
Ideas bouncing back and forth,
Which ones are the best?

XXX

Sun through the curtains
Gives the room a subtle charm
And turns dross to gold.

ANGEL IN AN URBAN LIGHT

The word was made flesh
And dwelt among us.
Urban ruins, rusty concrete walls
Surround a totemic figure
A tangle of wire and plastic
A beautiful face
Eyes closed, smiling
Facing the west
Setting sun
Nuclear light
Atoms.
It's all the same in the end
You, me, concrete, rust.
We end up the same.

XXXI

A dull-witted man,
Mean spirit, dead soul, walks past
And makes me feel sad.

XXXII

Salamander boy,
Swimming in the jewelled sea.
Red rays on blue glass.

XXXIII

Here in the attic
My picture, like Dorian Gray's,
Is getting older.

XXXIV

Princes debate and
Decide our fate. We are sheep,
In the fold or out.

XXXV

Beyond dead commerce,
There are still human beings
Thinking and talking.

THE SMALL HOURS

In the small hours
I stare death in the face
In the small hours
When you're half asleep
Dreams eat reality
And your troubles return
To haunt you like ghosts
In the small hours
That's when they come
Storming through your door
With snarls and shouts
Jerk you awake
And bundle you in sacking
Drag you into the night
And throw you to the floor
Of a dark van. Kick.
In the small hours
You wake and stare
Into the darkness
Wondering where you are
Or even who you are.
In the small hours
Questions rise in your dreams
And sink unanswered when you wake.
Life seems vague
In the small hours

XXXVI

Willow tree bending,
Gracefully sweeping the pond,
Sighing in the breeze.

XXXVII

Corporate dead soul
Lecturing in a meeting.
Sycophantic laughter.

XXXVIII

Such friendly phrases
Mask a deadly vicious soul.
He likes his secrets.

XXXIX

As today becomes
Tomorrow, I think about
Trying something new.

XL

All things come apart,
Falling into dust in time.
Inevitably.

NAPALM DRUNK

This morning I woke up
With the smell of Napalm in my nose.
My head hurt, and my mouth was dry.
Blinding light from the flat bright sky,
Pins and needles behind my eyes.
Too much drink last night, and quite
A lot of foolish talk.

Truth is in the wine, they say,
But It's rubbish. We all end up
Stupid when we're drunk.

XLI

A feather drifting.
A twig floating in the stream.
A wild goose flying.

XLII

Have we been careless?
There is a hole in the air,
And life is burning.

XLIII

Too many people
Going too fast and too far.
Not enough being.

XLIV

So many people
Crowding inside where it's warm.
Outside is empty.

XLV

I am jealous of those
Who have a clear vocation
From their day of birth.
What clarity and purpose
They can bring to their living!

NOVEMBER HAIKU

The harm that men do
When they give in to their greed
Is phenomenal.

His mouth is moving,
Words form and fall on my ears
But there's no sense there

An hour on the phone,
And nothing has changed at all
Except for the dust.

Republicans preach
Humanitarianism
While planning their war.

XLVI

Dumb stupidity,
Ugly, overt, cruel greed
Rules their existence.
Simple beauty leaves them cold.
Priceless is perhaps worthless.

XLVII

The pure grind of life
Gives me a rare pearl of luck
When I sense beauty
Shining clouded in shadow.
Treasure this moment for ever.

XLVIII

Attractive women,
Have an aura of their own.
They stand out in crowds
Drawing male eyes towards them
Unconcerned by their power.

XLIX

The lords of misrule
Sit in council at Easter,
Making senseless plans.

REMEMBER THE FEAR

Remember the fear you felt last night
When your heart was thumping
Your skin cold sweating
Stomach sour.

Your arms felt weak
Your brow felt cold
Your ears tingled
Your felt so old
The breath of death
Blew down your neck
And fear welled up
Inside you.

L

Corporate moron,
Babbling about stock value
While other folk starve

LI

Why does this man think
That I must think as he thinks?
I don't, so sod off.

LII

Tired, I lay in bed.
I didn't see the planets
Tonight, all lined up.

LIII

My window open,
I enjoy the gentle breeze.
A curtain flutters.

LIV

Avoiding the crowd,
I travel at night, alone.
At peace with myself.

DE CELESTIS

A fall of angels.
They fell to earth
In human form
With human souls
Tasting the bitter sweet
Fruit of human life.
Real dirt between their toes;
Aching bones and aging faces;
Joy and drunkenness;
Solitude, misery, pain;
Happiness and family.
The Tenth Order.

LV

You say irises -
So that's what they are, irises
in bloom, forever.

LVI

A prince of two lands
Master of neither, Concerned
With his own pleasure.

LVII

I had a vision
Of sleeping tigers waking,
Hunting in darkness.

LVIII

I watched a pebble
All day but it did nothing.
It was a pebble.

LIX

Enjoying the sun
Setting behind the houses.
Today tomorrow.

SEEKING SHELTER

Cloud over mountains
Brooding melancholy eyes
Staring at the ground

Distant quiet peace
A spirit ground in the dust
And a soul in flight

Hunted, despised. I
Need an angel to touch me
To balance my soul

LX

Storm blasting the road
Rain bulleting on the car
I drive carefully.

LXI

The last few metres -
I'm so glad to be back home -
Greeting my family.

LXII

Gentle rain falling
On the grass behind the house.
A drain chuckling

LXIII

The bell tolls gently
A distant reminder of church
A link with the past

LXIV

Rumble of the wind
Thick old branches rock and roll
In the mad old wood

BRIEFLY SNOW

Snow falls in one day
We throw snowballs and get warm
Snow melts the next day

NEVER SLEEP WITH ANGER IN THE AIR

A few short words
Before thinking
Temper engaged for
Seconds
Then hours of regret.

Shy apologies
Conversation over
A bottle of wine
A little laughter
Never sleep with
Anger in the air.

LXV

Faint whistle of wind,
Window rattling; yellow moon
Seen through drifting clouds

LXVI

Restless, ill at ease,
Age creeping into my bones -
I should be writing.

LXVII

Storm clouds and black trees
Seen from a chilly hillside
Where lonely sheep roam.

LXVIII

A fall of angels.
White blossom floats on the breeze,
And drops to the earth.

LXIX

Sleep is a blessing
Which helps to erase the pain
Of being alive.

ONE WINTER EVENING I WROTE THREE HAIKU

Night sky blade edge clear
Each star a cold drop of light.
Garden deserted.

My boy is angry.
He beats his fists on my knee,
Without knowing why.

Ice bound roots and soil
Amid the broken pieces
Of an old green pot

LXX

The dragon awakes.
Eyes glowing in the darkness,
He plans his escape.

LXXI

An old man sitting,
Staring at the infinite.
He is almost there.

LXXII

Old classic Basho,
Young innovative Basho,
Were the same person

LXXIII

No beauty today,
Or perhaps I fail to see
It in front of me.

A MESSAGE TO MY SON

I did and didn't believe my Dad
When he told me I would turn out bad.
Turns out he was neither wrong nor right
I wasn't a blessing, nor was I a blight.
He had his own ideas you see,
Though many made no sense to me.
I shouted "You just don't understand!",
Stomped and fumed in fury grand, but
Really he was sometimes wise and
Sometimes not in his replies.

So what's this message all about?
Only three, and already you shout,
Scream and kick, refuse to do
What your Mum and I ask you to.
I really don't want years of fight -
Distrust, lies, avoidance, dislike.
I love you and it makes me sad
To think that you might not like your Dad.
So I will always try and try again
To understand, to be your friend

LXXVIII

An honest man speaks,
Showing his humanity,
And I feel for him.

I wrote the snappily titled LXXVIII after hearing Falklands war veteran, a medic, talking about his experiences of the war and afterwards. People like him have been somewhere unimaginable, come out the other side, and now see everything through different eyes. They have a perspective and a quality that I will probably never experience personally.

LXXIX

The sparrow returns.
Where has he been for Winter?
It's good to see him.

RAGING LIKE DYLAN

Rage, rage against the dying of the light.
(Dylan Thomas)

Time flies by, ambition dying,
My wife crying, My boss lying
Like a bastard about everything.
The passion that once burned,
Turns inside me, dying,
A coal in the night, grows cold, no light.
When did the fire begin to die?
When did the lie begin to live?
My sin of omission -
Where did the anger go?
Where is that ambition
That flew in the face of
In-bred tradition, angrily spurning
All the mad bad old cold
Ways, whys and wherefores?
What political debate,
What agents of the state,
Can I hope to trust?
What religion, what business,
What council, what people?
Where is the light that once burned -
That fierce flame that licked
The edges of my soul and forced
Words of defiance from my mouth,
Raging against injustice, greed,
And the dying of the light.

LXXX

Clouds over Haarlem,
Dissident sun, weeping sky,
Child in a puddle.

LXXXI

Weary of travel,
I wish that change would slow down,
Just for a short while.

LXXXII

Bitter angry face
Staring through a car window,
Resenting the poor.

In London I saw a man in a BMW deliberately open his car door to bang against the knees of a poor migrant girl who was trying to wash his windscreen. This was at Hyde Park Corner, a crossroads in one of the wealthiest places on the Earth

LXXXIII

The backs of houses
Look much more lived in than the
Presentable fronts

MIDWINTER BLUE

Not a leaf in sight
Its dark at three
Ice on the road
Storms out at sea
Wind in the trees
Snow on the news
It's dark when I wake
With the midwinter blues

December 19, 2002

TWO SUITS

Sunlight with an edge
Tears a hole in the window
Bleeding golden light
Into this cube
Where two suits, no souls,
Two faces, no expressions,
Fence with words
And get nowhere.

LXXXIV

Green bushes, grey walls
Tall trees, squat homes with black slates,
Eggshell sky, no clouds.

LXXXV

Solace in friendship.
An evening spent talking
About everything.

LXXXVI

Old man in corner,
A little rock of content
In the turbulence

LXXXVII

To find real peace
You must reject everything
That causes discord.

LXXXVIII

I watched the light die -
Slow shadows creeping over
The garden, silence.

WINTER

Grey sky dripping rain
Alone in this gloomy room
I watch the drops fall

Snow suddenly falls
As thunder grows in the sky
Black bird on white snow

GHOST PETALS

Deep in the forest
A flower blooms in the night
Unusual, but true.
Nobody saw it happen,
And soon the flower was gone.

REGARDLESS

Grey winter
Dry cold road
A sudden spread of
Tiny yellow flowers
Turns my mood
From chill to warm
Life goes on
Regardless

LXXXIX

Old age and beauty,
Tranquillity in one face,
Youth in the other.

XC

A cry in the night,
Clear and remote, strangely sad,
Gone in a moment.

XCI

Swans on the river
Drifting silently along,
Absorbed in themselves.

XCII

The wind cursed and cried
Tearing with vicious fingers
At all earthbound things

XCIII

Grey dawn light, bag packed,
Son awakes, cries on the stairs,
But I must go now.

ONCE DUST

I fear the future
When I look into the past.
Man has not changed much.

To battle again.
Tomorrow the lines will form.
We fight for nothing.

Grass grows and grass dies.
Under a grey sky I stand
Watching the grass die.

Raining again, but
Quietly. Whispering in
The background. Silence.

Water bestows life
On this small black rock. Once dust,
Now it shines brightly.

XCIV

My curses on those
Who have wasted precious time,
Especially mine.

XCV

We make our own dreams,
Be they good, bad or boring.
They reflect our lives.

XCVI

WIND IN THE PINES, TWO VERSIONS

The wind in the pines,
A sigh from old mother Earth
As people flit by

People dart around,
The Earth heaves a heavy sigh -
The wind in the pines

Brem-sur-Mer, France

BAGHDAD

Baghdad was 'liberated' yesterday.

Excited teenagers
Topple the ugly statue,
Pound shoes on its head

Baseball bats thud down
On old regime informants
Who cower in the dust

April 11, 2003

XCVII

A moment like this
Holds a lifetime of content.
I hear the soft breeze

XCVIII

Sparrow in the tree
Drab little brown bird, singing
His heart out, joyful.

XCIX

Peace comes from action
As well as inaction. Soul
In a wooden sword

C

Breaking skys; my home
Squats under the waterfall.
Drama ends Summer.

A DAY IN THE LIFE

A hole in my face
Air whistling through the gap
Where my tooth should be

SB: Bad dream!
Me: What about? You haven't been to sleep yet.
SB: Outside is a bad dream

Young, imperious,
Stubborn, demanding, bright and
beautiful small boy;
Blonde hair always shining, his
Spirit burning like the sun.

An angel sleeping;
My hand under his fingers
Feels them slightly stir.

CI

Youth and passion strive
Through every passing season
To remain alive.

CII

This world I love, how
It's beauty overwhelms me;
Spirit of mankind.

CIII

Madness upon him
Coursing like a wild river
Through his unhinged mind

CIV

O speak now to me –
My prayers drift up through dull skies;
Sickly orange sun.

CV

A plain of nothing.
Desert to the horizon.
A drop of water.

MY GOD IS YOUR GOD

My God is your God
Is your Allah, is Yahweh
And all the many names of God
That men have used in time.

My God is your God.
I listen to him in my soul
Not to words of mortal men
Just his voice in me

My God is your God
Whether he exists or not.
Whether you like it or not.
We share one God

NIGHT

Burning midnight oil
A night bird mournfully hoots.
Solitary writing

IN TRANSIT

Airport early morning,
Reluctant journey.
Security search
Annoyed me -
Inadequate
Yet invasive.
Jumped a queue -
Was rude to a man.
Drank bad coffee,
Smoked once.
Walked to the gate,
Claimed my chair
From a woman
Sitting there.
Read Kerouac
Above the clouds -
Much like me
When it comes to
Haiku.
Experiment.
Be concise.
Rules are for guidance
Not blind obedience.
Use them in context.

FOR HIS NAME ALSO

For his name also is written in the book of life
(R S Thomas, Affinity)

O the joy of sitting waiting, while the chaos in his head
Works itself out slowly, and the penny drops like lead.

Is there a tiny spark of life back there behind his eyes?
Something must be working, to manufacture all his lies.

This poor young fool with his sleepless crazy face
Has sacrificed his soul to run ambition's race.

But don't forget his human birth - perhaps there's still a trace,
A deprecated, hidden crumb of innocent childlike grace.

HAMMERSMITH

Standing on Queen Caroline Street
My island in a river of steel,
I feel alone in this crowded place.
A deep breath of polluted air
Before risking the current.

Ragged bagged up bundles
Line the doorways of King St
Under the shadow of a fat bank
The silent homeless with empty
Polystyrene cups and blank eyes.

Rain under a hovering sky
Grey with the tears of sooty angels
I stood and smoked in the shadow
Of a grimy concrete monolith
Watching hurried lives in the rain.

WHAT JOY IS

Smile.
Today I saw
On the television
A downs syndrome child
Consumed with radiant joy
Listening to the beating of a drum

THE WAITING ROOM

Facing a white wall -
The corridor of power
Is awash with fog

In a high white room
Pretty women come and go -
Michelangelo

Monkeys chattering
Outside the open window -
I wish they would stop

An angel arrives,
Dressed in money and power.
Looking for someone.

All these things will pass,
Drifting into the dark night
Where the clocks have stopped.

BOB ARMSTRONG

I used to follow him round the garden,
Full of interest and trying to help;
"Where does rain come from?" I asked.
Bob smiled and stopped his work.

He cupped his hands to catch the rain,
And in his quiet old voice explained
How water rose up from the sea
And formed the clouds passing over me

He let me taste the fallen rain
"But the sea is salty!", I said, unsure,
"That's the miracle of it all -
God makes the rain fall down pure".

I was four at the time - Bob Armstrong was an old man who used to help my parents keep their garden in shape. This is based on one of my earliest childhood memories.

JANUARY SNOW

Snow billows around
Glistens wetly on the ground.
It will freeze tonight

Hailstones this morning,
Then an hour of wintry sun.
How I long for Spring!

CAIN'S PEOPLE

Have we ever lived in peace?
Has there ever been a time
When angry men did not release
The dogs of war? Will we ever
Realise that bombs and bugs,
Young sacrificial suicides
And bullets bought with deadly drugs
Will ultimately kill us all?

DEATH BY WATER

Walk into the river
Wash me clean of sin
Stand on sand and sing my song
While the shadows on the rocks grow long.
The ocean gleams
White waves cold seams
Light, green and glowing bright
The everlasting surge, alight.
How many deaths?
How many cold eyes
Have gazed unseeing in this place?
How many years have gone to waste?
I slept at last
And dreamt of shores
Where wanton boys pulled wings from flies
With godlike grace, and giggled as they died.
We speak of death
In jokes or whispers,
Wary of the taboo laid like tar
Upon this topic linked to tears.
We hardly pause
To think a while,
To contemplate this final friend,
Guaranteed to be there at the end.

WAY STATION

Tired, red-eyed and pale,
I trudge through the open door
And put down my bag

Late sun rays at dusk
Make moth-wings in dusty air
Happily flitting.

Shoes off by the door
Sitting sometimes dozing while
waiting for hot tea

Here have a thousand
Generations stopped to rest,
Polishing the wood

FOUR HAIKUS IN SUMMER

Bursting with giggles
He rolls off the couch and runs
Through the living room

Turn off the engine
A mantle of silence falls
Rare moment of peace

Walking there from here
I pass through somewhere else and
Like it just as much

Try to meditate
While sitting in a small tent
Just being alive

VENDEE

Sitting under pines,
Tall trunks, chaotic branches -
Smoking though I shouldn't.

This tiny cramped cabin
Is my home for a fortnight.
Drumming rain, tin roof.

Yesterday, I watched
The moon conquer the dark sky.
Basho moon viewing.

HAIKUS FROM HOME

Supine, glassy-eyed
Staring at a pale ceiling.
A dot with eight legs.

Claw-marked white muslin
Like parchment in the sunlight.
Eyes closed, nothing there.

I crushed a beetle,
Not on purpose - it was there,
Under my foot. Sad.

I would like to stop
Jumping like a jitterbug
And do my own thing.

IN NEED OF BED

Here I am in need of bed
The alcohol went to my head
I couldn't stand, and so I sat
Unfortunately upon the cat

With claw-marks in my drunken arse
I jumped and made some choice remarks
I crawled up twenty seven stairs
And went to sleep without saying prayers.

FIVE WINTRY HAIKU

Metallic sunlight
Streams across the waterland
To blank horizons.

Frost rims my window.
There, one ancient tree in a
Forest of saplings.

A drainage canal
Gleams like a katana laid
on a grey carpet.

Eyes, Reluctant tears,
Stinging in the whipping wind
Around the corner.

Even my northern blood
Runs colder on this plain
Between God and Earth

OLD NEW LABOUR

Angry young men grow old and grey
But do they ever fade away?
Does the anger seethe and churn
Underneath the politics they've learned?

Every day I hear them speak,
Idealists who no longer seek
A better, purer human world.
They're tired, betrayed, their values sold

To serve an ever-shrinking pride.
Now they join the winning side
Instead of following their belief.
Ideals are gone, and time's the thief.

JANUARY HAIKU

Lord grant me some time
To recompose my spirit
Pacify my soul

Moonlight on the grass
Cat walking in the shadows
Everything is grey

Prone, still, staring up
At the ceiling. Not a sound
In this darkened room

I am no angel
One of the fallen am I
A soul now human

Sleep, dream, wake, wash, eat.
Walk, sit, work, think, speak, eat, drink.
Lie, sleep, dream, sleep, dream.

FIRES

Fan the unforgotten flame
Until it rages like a wild fire.
My conscience pricks when e'er I think
Of my inaction, my complacent sloth.
O God! How can you love us still
When we elect such men to rule our lives.
Sound the trumpets, ring the bells,
Retie the ropes that leashed the dogs of war!
Yes, let the 'untamed fire of freedom'
Burn in every corner of our world!
Let every person have a chance
Of liberty, peace and equal rights;
A chance to live in dignity, and
See their sons and daughters laugh and love.
When you release those martial dogs
You place a further curse upon our race.
Eye for eye and tooth for tooth -
The biblical cycle of revenge.
O our resolve is firm - we fight,
But in that fight we generate more hate.

THE TOMB OF GHENGIS KHAN

The trees stand proud, cast
Leafy shadows on the forest floor.
A horseman reigns his horse, dismounts and
Sits down on the grass.
He watches as a hunting bird drops
Down into the bracken,
Then rises back with clattering wings and
Struggling squeaking prey.

In such a place lies Genghis Khan,
Secreted at his death.
His life, his flesh, his might, all gone
Enshrined within the Earth.
A hundred horses trampled flat
The surface of his tomb .
Imperial guards watched growing grass,
As thirty years ticked by.

GETTING FORGETFUL

Today I forgot a lot of stuff.
I mixed my letters when I typed,
Went upstairs to find a thing
But couldn't remember what it was.
I walked back down and looked around
- remembered what it was and went
Back up the stairs to find the thing
But couldn't remember it again.

I called my Mum and told her this -
You're getting older dear, she said.
Is this normal Mum? I asked -
O yes dear, soon you'll lose your head.
Well thanks Mum, that's a help, I whined -
No problem son, she said, then laughed -
I expect one day you'll lose your mind
And everyone will think you're daft

Thanks Mum

ENTROPIC HAIKU

Consumed with sadness
Age crumbling my memories
Into loose fragments

A pallid petal
Broken loose from a long stem
Stranded on cold gravel

Darkness and silence
Seep through my empty house
Missing my children

A lonely whisper
As the wind strokes the branches,
White blossom falling

Skin like old parchment
Tells it's own long story, but
His eyes are still young.

BOXING DAY HAIKU

A rock in my bag,
Reminds me of many things.
It's not just a rock

Boxing Day, December 2005

HAIKU FOR NOW IN AUTUMN

Pond reflecting trees,
Leaden sky touching dead earth.
Feeling monochrome.

A flight of wild geese
Congregates by the water
For a few moments.

Too few daylight hours.
I wake slowly in darkness
While the birds migrate.

Haarlemmermeer, November 2005

JOURNAL HAIKU

A land of plenty
With many starving people;
One fattened ruler.

I cried at the rain
Dripping from black wet branches;
Basho spoke of tears.

O what a freedom!
A chevron of wild geese, high,
Dark in the pale sky.

Pale and perfect skin,
Glowing faintly in moonlight;
Asleep and smiling.

My death waits for me,
A sullen exacting god
With an unkind heart.

A rose in winter;
No flower, but thorns to cast
My blood on white snow

A piece of me, yes;
The cold east wind has frozen
the rest. I am ice.

A scabby hotel
In a nameless part of France;
I want to go home.

AGE UNCOMMUNICATED

In a bed in a corner
Lay the old man alone
On the floor at his side
Lay an unplugged phone
His breath was slight
His eyes were closed
He'd lost all contact
With his toes.
Behind his face
His ticking brain
Relived the high points
Of his life again.

FOUR HAIKU IN THE WIND

The wind is strong. The forecast was for gales today, and I can see trees shaking. It is raining heavily, so that Jamie and I walked with umbrellas to school. He sang 'singing in the rain' and twirled his umbrella. I like the wind and the rain.

Pink petals dropping
Riding the angry raindrops
On the swirling wind

Driving rain hammers
The fishmongers cold window.
The dead fish don't care

So many cars parked
Under the trees. Each one has
A wreath of petals

Black crow rides the wind;
He loves to soar and dive bomb
Struggling cyclists.

RED DUSK AND THE DARK PRINCE

Light flickers, ripples
With the waves as they wander
Across the shoreline

Red dusk calms the sea
Washes blood-like across the
Dusty white sand dunes

He sees death riding
Towards him. A master thief
Come to take his soul

The dark prince of greed
Feeds his aching emptiness
With dull, tainted gold

When the stream runs dry
I will walk across the dead
Wasteland, without tears.

A VISITOR IN JAPAN

Shinjuku Station;
A lonely black crow flaps past
Shadowed mirror glass

Dragonfly sitting
On ancient rock, darts away;
Moss and lichen cling.

Tokugawa shrine;
Peaceful forest place where the
Dead and quick commune

Sunlight streams freely
Through the pines, dancing on the
Tomb of a Shogun

We pause, sip water
From copper cups, gazing at
The Yomeimon gate

So many live souls
Moving in waves; bright blooming
Neon - Shibuya.

New green rice; old graves.
Families embedded here
For generations

IN LIMBO

Swans asleep in a
A lake reflecting midnight;
His lost soul stirring.

Grey mist hanging low
Over the broken concrete;
Automobile ghosts

BEATENBERG

All things Change
So Daisen said
As he looked at the river

In these clouds
I see the same
Change without ending

Even the peaks
Will be brought down,
Ground into sand and washed

Down the river
To the endless sea
Where it all began.

But for now I see
These ancient rocks
Scored with icy claws

In my brief life
I will enjoy and
Praise these giants

And they will remain
More or less the same

MY SON ASKS ME WHY

There are mean old men
In a mean old world

My son asks me why
The wise old men
Don't leave me be
So I can play with him

My son asks me why
The Sun is so hot
Birds fly in the sky
And the stars are all dots

My son asks me why
God lets us get ill
Why some folk are poor
And others are cruel

My son asks me why
Plants grow up green,
Why trees are all different
And some kids are mean

My son asks me why
He was born when he was
And I hold him up high
And I say 'just because'

My son asks me why
I am two metres tall
Which is not what I am
It's just that he's small

My son whispers why
Do you go to your work?
Please stay here at home, Dad.
God, leaving him hurts.

SOULS IN ASHES

Bright-lit coloured screens of crap
A thousand channels down the wire
Deluge data, swarms of words
And everybody lies and lies

What's real what's false, the shaded zone
We live within; We live we lie
And sometimes die in televised wars
Where both sides howl victorious cries

The dream within, the life without;
Souls in ashes, bottled rage
Spills out and cuts the veins of boys,
Released to find another cage

What beauty, dirty and corrupt,
With morals lost and conscience gone;
Our history is a tattered flag,
Forgotten on a library wall
Where no-one sees it any more.
Pro patria mori, what have we done?

THE OLD BARN

Bent old wooden beams
Will hold up the roof for a
Few hundred years more

Wood pigeon flops down
On the grass in front of me;
One wary eye glints.

Wheat and dust; stubble,
Green and gold, harvest sunlight.
Sitting on warm stones.

END OF DAYS

I am a dark beast,
At war with my own spirit.
The light is fading.

Into the abyss
I stare with starting horror;
Emptiness. The end.

LYRIC ON SLEEP

Oh that this too too solid flesh would melt
Thaw and resolve itself into a dew;
(William Shakespeare, Hamlet)

I want sleep again, and now.
Escape the daily grind of life.
Not death, but dreams I will allow
To help me flee from toil and strife.
In sleep I lose the need to think -
My mind has no need to wish to hide.
It needs no pilot at the helm.
No stress, no pressure, no need to decide.
My mind asleep never gets bored,
Never has to finish chores.
Relentless living leaves me tired,
And sleep is all that I desire.
But in that sleep what awful dreams
Might come? And what would they mean?
Better not to sleep the sleep of flight
Better by far to stand and fight.

SOLD

Black flowers of evil
Grow in his soul
He sold himself
To reach his goals.

He is dollar rich
But spirit poor,
Has no more morals
Than a door.

He talks of freedom
Speaks of dreams
And cynically leads
His corporate team.

Their greed is great
But they don't care
If wealth creation
Lays the world bare.

THREE BROTHERS

One brother knew how to do everything
But did nothing
And knew why

One brother knew how to do nothing
And did nothing
Very well

One brother knew how to do little
But did everything
Anyway

LAST DAY OF AUGUST

A Summer bee
Flew past me
O how nice
It was to see
And hear this
Little chap.
Someone had said
That bees were dead,
That all our waste
Had killed them off.
So it was good to see
This Summer bee.

ON THE RETURN OF FORGOTTEN MEMORIES

Memories fell on me like a shower of shrapnel
and I relived the awful moment of floor-rooted
Embarrassment.

Memory returned and left a sentimental glow
Which warmed me, and left me thinking
Of my childhood

Lost memories hovered moth-like at the window
Of my consciousness. Try as I might,
I could not reach them.

Awful shaking came upon me as my memory
Of a sudden almost-death stabbed out like
Broken mirror shards

Memory unexpected, revelationary return
Of the forgotten moment when I realised
That love exists

These fading memories. Frustration as I grasp
At the fraying edge of a lost time
And it disappears.

And I grieve
(though lightly
Because I cannot
Remember
What I have lost)

BUSINESS MEETING

The boredom eats into my head
My body lives, my soul feels dead.
A talking head drones on and on
And gestures feebly at the screen;
The Airco desiccates our skin.
My fingers clutch a ballpoint pen -
With magic grace they move it's point
In doodling drifts across the page.
In all those random shapes I see
Another strange reality.
My wandering mind with wanton grace
Flees the tedium of this place, and
Finds a realm of sight and sound
Where poets and musicians abound and
Dancing girls with mobile hips
Giggle as they jiggle their tits.
The great lord, magnificently drunk,
Stands and shouts his latest verse;
The scent of opium, like rotten blooms,
Drifts to every corner of the room.
"Any questions?" I hear him ask.
My head rears up, my face a mask
Which hides my boredom and the fear
That I have absolutely no idea
What this stupid meeting was about.
I keep my peace and then go out.

RHYMING COUPLETS

Here in my house at the end of the lane
I watch the everlasting rain

Together we build a palace of dreams
Of lego blocks and lego beams

In the train the people come and go
And slump in their seats like lumps of dough

Grim-faced fat man sprawled in sleep
From shaven head to sports shoe feet

A Lady in a purple scarf
Looks as if she never laughs

Gormless child with PSP
Sitting on his father's knee

Land of glory, land of hope
Land of people who can't cope

The Sun is gone, the clouds loom low
The road's awash, the traffic slow

FOUR WINTER HAIKU

No leaves on the tree;
Branches like broken fingers
Claw at the grey sky.

Pale and consumptive,
The feeble sun creates a
Watery shadow.

I blow on my hands;
Breath like smoke, a hint of warmth.
I forgot my gloves.

Tired yellow rose
Still clinging to a lean stem
On midwinter day.

DEATH AND AN OLD POET

Stranded far from home
Moonlight gleams through the cracked roof
I am Ink on paper

Red petals of blood
Each one a shock to my soul.
Why does death seek me?

My flesh will corrupt,
Becoming dust, flying far
On the constant wind

My fellow pilgrim
Sits by me, talking. Soon my
Dreams will fade away.

From nothing we come.
Blessed with life for a few years,
Then where do we go?

For life is sublime.
Nothing has greater value -
The image of God.

My bony fingers,
Stiff with age, rest in his hand
As he reads to me

The images fade.
My eyes have seen a thousand
Stories acted out.

Here in this broken
House, I find my final words.
To live is to love.

'Death and an Old Poet' was written in 2005 in London, Amsterdam and Tokyo, and flights going between them.

This is one of my favourite poems of recent years. The language pleases me, and I enjoy the juxtaposition of the Haiku form with topics which are somewhat eastern in style while retaining the western flavour which comes from me. It recalls a little the fact that Matsuo Basho, one of the most famous of Japanese Haiku poets, died far from home when he was on his travels.

www.ingramcontent.com/pod-product-compliance
Ingram Content Group UK Ltd.
Pitfield, Milton Keynes, MK11 3LW, UK
UKHW041935190726
13854UKWH00004B/1602

9 781847 996732